# Gentle Flower Growing Wild

Fartema M. Fagin

WALDENHOUSE PUBLISHERS, INC.
WALDEN, TENNESSEE

## Gentle Flower Growing Wild

Copyright © 2016 by Fartema Mae Fagin (1950) All rights reserved. No part of this book may be reproduced in any form, or by any means, electronic or mechanical, including photocopying, recording, or any information browsing, storage, or retrieval system, without permission from the author.

ISBN: 978-1-935186-79-3

Library of Congress Control Number: 2016910868

"A collection of 46 poems reflected through the eyes of the author that describes layers of emotions based on interpersonal relationships. The poems are inspirational and hopeful, and they paint vivid pictures of some life experiences that helped develop, grow and shape the author's character." -- provided by Publisher

Published by Waldenhouse Publishers, Inc.

100 Clegg Street, Signal Mountain, Tennessee 37377 USA

888-222-9229   www.waldenhouse.com

Printed in the United States of America

## *DEDICATION*

To the memory of my parents
Lefes and Annie Mae (Phillips) Bray
who gifted me with a thirst for the written word
and a love for language

To my gifted sons
Peter Darrin Ledbetter and Alton DeWayne Ledbetter
and Family and Friends
who encouraged this collection of inspired work

# *Preface*

Like a captured bird, the freedom to express is limitless even by the physical constraints of a cage. The spirit of a captured bird can still ring out in song. Poetry is a tool which unlocks the mind to a treasure of thoughts waiting to be expressed. Poetry is an act of self-discovery. Creative writing is an outlet that gives me an opportunity to express, discover, and rediscover the who that I am.

I find myself engaging my writing skills whenever and wherever the "muse" visits me. My genre of writing includes poetry, essays and short stories. In addition, journaling is a practice which allows me the opportunity to express my deepest thoughts.

## *Table of Contents*

| | |
|---|---:|
| Preface | v |
| My Mother's Garden | 9 |
| Angel in Silver Sneakers | 10 |
| Shoes for the Journey | 11 |
| The Blessing | 12 |
| The Thorn in Her Side | 13 |
| Face of a Clown | 14 |
| Two Lace Dresses | 15 |
| Shadows | 16 |
| Salt | 17 |
| Endangered Species | 18 |
| Beyond the Red Door | 19 |
| Watermarked | 20 |
| Sometimes You Can't Help Who You Love | 21 |
| Wasted | 22 |
| Treasure Chest | 23 |
| For Those Who Stayed Behind | 24 |
| The Power of a Kiss | 25 |
| Dawning Grace | 26 |
| Sweet Tunes Brought to Life | 27 |
| Cracked House | 28 |
| In Search of Rhythm | 30 |
| Cactus In the Desert | 31 |

| | |
|---|---|
| Play Me Like a Piano | 32 |
| A Domestic Noose | 33 |
| Death Loses It's Sting If You | 34 |
| They Say Love is Blind | 35 |
| A Handful of Love | 36 |
| Red Dress Affair | 37 |
| Dancing With My Muse | 38 |
| Love Stands By | 39 |
| Salve for the Soul | 40 |
| In the Garden | 41 |
| Cinderella Slippers | 42 |
| People of the Pines | 43 |
| Dream Lover | 44 |
| Disposable Dolls | 45 |
| Windblown | 46 |
| Light Sugar | 47 |
| Candle Lights and Fireworks | 48 |
| Wind Songs | 49 |
| Bags for Life | 50 |
| Raw Emotions in a Basket | 51 |
| Water Lily | 52 |
| Chasing Bubbles | 53 |
| Pigs Gone Crazy | 54 |
| Ripen to Death | 55 |
| About the Author | 57 |

# *My Mother's Garden*

She took a plot of land,
Raised up a house for God.
Planted hymns and praise,
Her produce was love.

## *Angel in Silver Sneakers*

An Angel in her
Silver sneakers
Dancing for Jesus
Smiling and twirling
Free from pain
Stars twinkling
Lighting her pathway
Stretch for the Son
Love heals All.

## *Shoes for the Journey*

White high top walkers with black dye trimmed soles,
Training boot for babies taking that first step of life.
Keds, Adidas, Sneakers, Nikes,
Cletes for the feet,
Air Jordans to jump hurdles.
Black and white saddle oxfords,
White poodle dogs swinging on a pink circle skirt.
Blue suede shoes made for dancing and swiveling hips.
Brown rugged brogues as sturdy as combat boots,
No glass slipper fairy tale dreams for this Princess,
Or magical trips in ruby red shoes on the yellow brick road.
Black patent leather shoes moonwalking on the stage,
Purple high heels strutting to the tunes from an electric guitar.
Doves sitting in a high wire weeping a blessing
About to take place in a small country church.
A reluctant bride in a white lace trimmed dress,
Creeps up the aisle in white satin heels,
Joining her helpmate in his black shiny spectators,
As they prepare to waltz through a course of matrimony.

## *The Blessing*

Hold fast to this beautiful gift,
Marriage is a sacred treasure
Where love nurtures the soul.

Hold fast through times
Of joy and sorrow
On this journey called life.

Hold fast and let the Creator
Shine his light upon you
To light your path.

Hold fast as He pours out
Showers of blessings
According to His plans.

## *The Thorn in Her Side*

She visited the well daily
As she drew water to quench her thirst,
Clean the open wounds.
A painful reminder from broken promises.
She suffered alone and in silence,
Her spirit ran dry and empty as she thirsted for healing.
Her broken heart burdened
Under the weight of a trail of tears.
Her soul ached for a love she failed to find.
She longed for a 'happily-ever-after-life'
Her fairy tale dreams crushed
Again and again.
Abandoned and alone at the well
A stranger approached her.
He too wanted service from her,
And in exchange offered a new way of life
To quench her thirst, heal her brokenness,
And feed her hunger.
She trusted Him with her barren and broken heart,
And in exchange she found an everlasting love
Enduring the pain of the thorn in her side
She found forgiveness and strength in His love.

## *Face of a Clown*

Many species of fish
Living a life of wonder
Color the ocean's bottom
With beautiful splendor.

A lonely clown fish
Missed the calm blue sea
Frowned around in a tank,
Looking to find a way to flee.

Out of its natural habitat
Among the other species he glowed.
He was the most colorful of all,
Stretched its fins and rowed.

Bright vibrant colored stripes,
Searched for a way to flee
The clown fish longed to find
His smile reflected in the sea.

## *Two Lace Dresses*

Her remains were lowered into the dust of the earth
From which she came.
A part of me went into the dark hole with her.
After a short period of absence from my life,
My heart slowly turned to fossil.
A fading childhood memory clouded my view,
As she unwrapped two lace dresses.
One a powder blue like the sky,
The other the color of sand.
The lace pattern represented the fragility of life.
Her home-going attire
As she anticipated her journey to a place called heaven.
A Cinderella ball must have danced in her head,
As she waited for the clock to strike the end of time.

## *Shadows*

As darkness engulfs the day,
Soft shadows play on the lamp posts,
Lining the streets.
Trees taking refuge from the light of day.
Shadows fading into the darkness of the night.
As people from all walks of life encounter
Trials and carry them on their journey
In the softness of shadows,
Subdued by a measure of light,
A gentle softness like a halo,
Blurred edges of a dark shadow
Embraced by the light,
Shadows softly creeping into the darkness,
Seeking joy in the morning.

## *Salt*

Take time to explore,
And find more joy in life,
Taste what it means
To be the salt that sweetens the pie,
Or the seasoning that flavors the meat.
To toil the soil and plant the seed.
Nourish the growth on which to feed.
To gather the harvest from the fruit of labor,
Keep moving, serving and sharing life's best.
Spreading salt to flavor and preserve life.

## *Endangered Species*

Confused and filled
With self-hate and shame
Hey Youngblood,
What's this game?

Crippled with diseases,
In need of a cure
And now they say
You're an endangered species.

Castrating and killing,
Rupturing the lives
Of families and children
Just trying to survive.

Demand a plan,
In the courts or off,
Let's make a stand
To save the man.

## *Beyond the Red Door*

Up in a high rise break room with a bird's eye view below,
My eyes rest on a sanctuary in the middle of a parking lot.
A large scarlet red door summons my weary soul.
The fancy carved stonework forms a gothic structure.

One day I will enter through the bold red door.
Search among the pillars to the mysteries within.
Red is the color of happiness to the people of the China.
A pulsating heart full of joy pumping red blood cells of life.

Beyond the scarlet red door, I picture a cathedral ceiling,
A long, winding wood crafted alter, curved and stained pews.
Moments of solitude escape me with more hours left to labor,
Time to get back to work and share in the bread of life.

## *Watermarked*

Time ticked away too soon,
Countless hours shared
Quietly sifted away like sand in an hour glass.
Each grain represented
A moment of joy,
A moment of pain,
A moment of praise,
A moment of gain,
A measure of hope,
A measure of rain,
A measure of growth,
A measure of distance.
Marked our days spent with fond memories,
Tear marked tattoos,
Etched into the cornerstone of my soul.

## *Sometimes You Can't Help Who You Love*

Thoughts of our yesterdays,
Made my heart pine for more.
The memories we built in love as one.
Filled my lonely nights.
Until one day you called me in distress,
Your voice bridged the distance
Said your life was in a mess.
I gathered up the fragments of my broken heart,
And placed them at your feet,
Nothing now to keep us apart.
Reunited we danced to our love songs,
The timing seemed so right
But then the shattered pieces fell apart
In the middle of the night.

## *Wasted*

Tears flooded
And broke the walls of her heart,
Her heart pumped gallons of salt water tears.
The emptiness exposed
A wasteland of pain.
In the absence of her heart,
A tombstone marked the spot.

## *Treasured Chest*

Search your bags for me,
A part of my heart is gone.
I cannot break free
From this lingering pain.

Praying to be your invited guest,
So I may search among your parts,
Roam about your treasured chest,
To reclaim a missing part of my heart.

## *For Those Who Stayed Behind*

A great migration took flight,
Like a flock of blackbirds headed south.
Only these birds headed up north
In search of a right to humanity
To escape the cold and cruel
Jim Crow climate of the south.
Many were led to believe that
The North was the Promised Land.

Generations of families loaded up
Their broken down bodies and sagging spirit,
Precious few possessions in exchange
For Promises of a better life.
Some rooted souls stayed behind,
Farmers, preachers, teachers and prophets,
Warriors who fought the forces,
And endangered their existence.

Armed with a sense of pride,
They bravely fought struggles courageously.
Preserving and saving souls against prosecutions
For being black and even treated as game.
Souls were baptized in creeks and riverbeds
Which flowed with the blood and sweat of our forefathers,
Those who stayed behind secured a place for us to call home.

## *The Power of a Kiss*

Your lips felt like a cool liquid fluid,
Poured carefully over briskets of hot coals.
Picture perfect lips,
Full and voluptuous
Promising pleasure.

As our lips met, sparks ignited
And produced a chemical combustion.
Red hot blazes licked at the ceiling of my soul.
Hearts pounded like the sound of drums.
Paradise discovered between your lips and mine.

## *Dawning Grace*

The lake sparkled in the early dawn,
Inviting me to test its miraculous powers.
Slowly I unfurled my down covers,
And wandered to the edge of the lake.

Across the mirrored lake,
A new horizon greets me.
I glide gracefully into the body of water,
Ripples mark my path to a new dawn.

## *Sweet Tunes of Life*

Hopscotch, jump rope, no need for a toy,
Simple childhood games brought us lots of joy.
You sketched beautiful cartoons,
Sang soulful hymns and spiritual tunes.
We shared many fears and tears,
Throughout those bittersweet years.
You shared your wisdom of the Word,
In order to serve as a sword.

## *A Cracked House*

Damp, dirty and stinkin'
The smell crawled up my nose.
And settled in my nostrils.
My eyes took in the sights,
Of what used to be called home.

A naked dim light bulb,
Dangled from the ceiling,
A colorless wall surrounded me.
Served as a backdrop to artwork,
Hanging nondescript, but visible.

Worn sofas anchored the room,
Old dingy blankets littered about,
To provide comfort from the cold,
Or a cushion for the body,
Remnants of what used to be home.

I scouted out a place to sit,
As I held the baby close,
Wondered how an innocent baby
Could survive in such a mess,
That was once a loving home.

Her mother gathered some clothing,
Mindlessly moved about,
Stuffed them in a garbage bag,
Not caring to even know
That this house was once a home.

My heart settled in my throat,
Choking back stifled tears,
I cradled the baby to my chest,
To ward off the evil wills
Of a home that now broken, cracked.

## *In Search of Rhythm*

Flames licked at the black cast iron kettle,
Nestled and suspended high over the burning cinder blocks
In the black tile framed fireplace.
"The love I have for you burns so strong,"
He professed to her.
Likening it to trials of fire.
Metal alloy seared into gold.
Steadfast and strong, withstanding the test of time.
A medley of old blues filled the warm sacredness in the room.
Two cuckoo clocks winded with age ticked against time
In search of a rhythm,
As the flames from the fireplace danced silently
to the rhythm.

## *Cactus in the Desert*

A dry and desolate desert,
Windswept dust particles,
Tumbleweeds tossing about,
The only sign of visible life,
An earth colored lizard,
Sliver for cover beneath a rock.
Seeking refuge from the hot scorching sun.
Prickly needles on a lone green cactus.
A ghastly permanent shadow,
Stabbed into the sand, boughs stretched upward,
Pleading for an escape from Hell.

## *Play Me Like a Piano*

Tickle the ivories
And create in me a song.
A sweet sounding melody,
Full of romantic notes.

Let your fingertips
Roam and kiss the keys,
That keep my heart
In tune to your harmony.

## *A Domestic Noose*

Somewhere along the way,
With no map for a guide,
Two souls lost their direction,
Honor slipped away with trust.

A disease called disrespect
Set up shop in the home
And filled the stale air with vile,
toxic vapors.

Dropped a rope of despair,
That hung in a noose,
To choke off any remnants of love,
Straining and struggling to breathe.

## *Death Loses Its Sting If You......*

Look for me in the rainbow,
Where you'll find beauty after the storm.
Feel me in the breeze of the wind,
As I gently nudge you through life's trials.
Seek the warmth of the sun rays,
I will embrace you in the light of my love.
Let the raindrops fall and touch the dry spirits
All the while cleansing your soul.
Give me a smile as beautiful as a rose,
So that you can feel my love reflected through you.

# *They Say Love is Blind*

Driven by the pain of loneliness,
Blindly seeking guidance
Around and away from the
Entrapments of life.

In a stupor she paces the floor,
The creaking sounds from the
Loose wooden boards,
Bears her pain and cries with her.

The walls fail to embrace her,
She stalks the streets at night.
Stumbling about wandering,
Sightless without a dog.

Searching for a lost love,
To light the dark pathways.
This dark familiar territory
Closing in like a vacuum.

## *A Handful of Love*

Allow me to hold your hands,
Again.
And feel the softness,
Caress
Your fingers in my hand.
Lean
Long and sensitive,
Strong.
Tapered nails trimmed to
Perfection.
Perched to give and receive
Love.
Feel the flow between us,
Kiss,
Planted wetly on your fingertips,
Seed,
Nurture and let it grow.

# *A Red Dress Affair*

Simple and elegant,
Nothing else would do.
The red dress I wore
When I gave my heart to you.

We danced the night away,
Made the music our own.
After all the rhythm and rhyme,
I found myself alone.

Colored with admiration,
An affair of the heart.
Explosion of affection,
Somehow it fell apart.

Cupid's arrow missed
The intended target.
The red dress is now only
A figment of my imagination.

## *Dancing with My Muse*

The pen takes control and finds itself steadily poised
in my hand,
Gliding across the blank pages,
Words beg to be expounded upon.
Consumed with a passion for writing I have
no other recourse.
My goal is not a measure of fame or my name
in neon lights,
Even though I would welcome such a plight.
Bestowing me with fortunes I would travel far and near,
Indulge in pleasurable portions of richness.
I would have a menu for fun in each and every season.
A popcorn garland of words strung together,
Gracing a tree of lights and ornaments.
Harmonious compositions in a song and dance
of simple pleasures,
A testimony to the beauty found in the gift of life.

## *Love Stands By*

Love is my heart fluttering
Each time we meet.
I tell it to be calm and cool,
And please don't skip a beat.

Love is the freedom to
Share your space.
Stir up your spirit and
Pull a smile across your face.

Love is my gift to you,
I hope that you will keep
Anchored in your heart,
As something very deep.

## *Salve for the Soul*

You asked for my hand,
I entrusted my life to you.
Hypnotized by your charm.
Our brown eyes found each other's soul,
Mirrored a mutual desire to be loved.
A magnetic charge drew us closer,
Softened the hard places.
Ruled by nature our love blossomed
Into a silent promise of eternal love.
Now in your absence I look for solace
In the memory of you loving me,
And me loving you back.

.

## *In the Garden*

The path was mysteriously inviting,
Together we ventured into the luscious rain forest.
Bravely and proudly I walked beside you,
Head held high like a Queen beside her King.
There was no fear of the love offerings.
Our taste buds delightfully enticed
By an abundance of fresh fruit.
Dew drops glistened on the green foliage,
Moist images blurred our vision.
Lured by the fragrant atmosphere,
We approached a clearance and found a stream
Dotted with pebbles of various sizes.
Like children at play we followed the flow,
Which fed into a nearby waterfall.
I slipped and fell deeply in love as you followed.
No need of a rescue mission plan,
As tracks of love resting quietly in the heart.

## *Cinderella Slippers*

The clear and shiny shoes sparkled
Under the bright glare of lights
In Rich's shoe department.
Shoes befitting a Princess

Revolving and spinning around
On the dance floor,
I envision myself as a Princess
At the Ball with my Prince.

A fancy pair of red slippers caught my eye,
I saw Dorothy click her heels three times.
Having been swept away to strange a land
The magical shoes carried her home.

## *People of the Pines*

Grounded in the red Georgia clay,
He planted four small pines.
Representing their roots.
He personalized them by name,
James Jesse, Lapharis and Robert,
Four brothers reaching toward the sky.
Standing straight and tall
Like steel flagpoles of varying size.
Holding red white and blue star spangled banner
Waving bravely in the wind.
Patriotism, perseverance and service
For home free range on open land.

## *Dream Lover*

Miracles happen every day,
That's what Luther croons.

Last night I dreamed you held me
In the tender folds of your arms.
I was as helpless as a piece of silly putty
In a child's hand at play.

Miracles happen every day,
That's what Luther croons.

Your spirit joined me this night,
Felt your moist lips upon mine,
Your embrace as warm as
A down filled comforter.

Miracles happen every day,
That's what Luther croons.

Melodious thoughts of us
Dancing on the edge of ecstasy.
Too soon the music stops
The thrill fades into the night.

## *Disposable Dolls*

Sad droopy eyes search day after day,
Cries of despair fill the room.
Robbed of their childhood,
The sweet sound of laughter lost.
Abandoned like broken and discarded toys,
Disposable as a soiled diaper,
Children neglected and in need of love.

## *Windblown*

Here I stand accused and acquitted.
"You just want to draw strength from me."
"Yes," I confessed, "I do."
Somehow you fooled me into believing
You had enough love to share.
Reject me now if you must.
But know this much I say,
"The strength I drew from you
Sustained me in the storm."

## *Light Sugar*

Pure love crystallized and glazed,
Shiny stars suspended in the universe,
Giving light to the love we shared.
Sugar crystals sprinkled in the sky.

## *Candle Lights and Fireworks*

Formal dining in Chastain Park
Illuminated a soft glow at each setting
Created an atmosphere of romance.
Stars played peek-a-boo,
In the depths of the dusky blue sky.
Musical bars of magic filled the air.
The symphony serenaded the patrons
With a melody of classical tunes,
A colorful array of fireworks burst
Through the sky and rained down
An aura of magical power.

# *Wind Songs*

Wildflowers dotted the hillside,
Pink, purple and red;
Yellow dandelions sprinkled about
A lush green carpeted playground.

Three little girls scrambled about,
Chasing butterflies.
Making it a game of play
For a fun filled day.

Giggling about sweet nothings,
Angel toes trample the soft grass below,
Chasing after their dreams,
With the wind carrying their songs.

## *Bags for Life*

A diaper bag draped over her shoulder,
Baby in her arms.
A toddler wobbles along beside her,
A happy face backpack dances on her back.

A teenager tripping off to school,
Book bag trailing on wheels.
A newly wed beginning a new life,
Matching bags for the honeymoon.

For some it is off to war to serve,
Mean green Army duffel bags
Stuffed and filled with gear
To fight a war for the promise of freedom.

## *Raw Emotions in a Basket*

She came to me seeking a safe place
Emptied herself as she became a fragile shell.
Heaving at every breath she gasped for air
As she fell into my arms of comfort.

Where was the woman I used to know?
A woman of courage and strength,
Self-assured and full of faith;
Now a basket case before my eyes.

I held her like a baby in my arms,
Muffled her sobs in my bosom,
Rocked her until she could find,
The rhythm to breathe on her own.

He was her knight in shining armor,
She entrusted him with her heart,
Assaulted now to a breaking point.
Needed – Oxygen to live again.

## *Water Lily*

Rarely cherished for its beauty,
Surrounded by a small body of water,
Sometimes shadowed by weeping willows,
I invite you into my wilderness,
Where my water lily blooms.

## *Chasing Bubbles*

Created from a breath of air,
Bubbles, bubbles, bubbles,
Wearing the colors of the rainbow,
Glistening before your eyes,
Give chase and catch one if you can,
For our life span is as short as a lifetime,
Or as long as a memory.

## *Pigs Gone Crazy*

Anger and bitterness boiled inside,
Cooked up poison vapors.
Hate spewed out and spread,
Tainting others in its path.
Attacked innocent victims.
Even the pigs in the book of Matthew
Refused to digest the hatred.
The crazy pigs squealed
And ran off to a sentence of
Death and destruction.

## *Ripen to Death*

Rotten fruit dangled from the tree limbs,
Clinging to a life of uncertainty.
Lying beneath the tree a bed of spoiled fruit
Blanketing the soil from which it came.

Mixed with the debris of rocks and twigs,
Bodies of apples embedded in the soil,
Filled the hot air with a suffocating stench.
Bodies of apples embedded in the soil,
Mother Nature bearing and burying her own.

## *About the Author*

Fartema (Ledbetter) Fagin is an adjunct professor and currently lives in Chattanooga, Tennessee. Her writing journey started as an active member of the International Women's Writing Guild. She has attended summer writing workshops sponsored by the Guild at Skidmore College, Saratoga Springs, NY, and Brown University in Providence, RI. While living in Georgia she was a representative for the Guild, and facilitated creative writing workshops in and about the community of metropolitan Atlanta.

Fartema has earned recognition for her poems from the National Poetry Society. She has also received awards from Clark Atlanta University, Atlanta, Georgia (English Department/Community Writing Essay Contest). Fartema has a bachelor's degree in English/Journalism from Georgia State University, Atlanta, Georgia and a master's degree in English Rhetoric from the University of Tennessee Chattanooga.

Goudy Old Style and Baker Script on LSI 50# Créme White
Type and Design by Karen Paul Stone

www.ingramcontent.com/pod-product-compliance
Lightning Source LLC
Chambersburg PA
CBHW030005050426
42451CB00006B/123